MW00679116

The
LAW
and
GRACE
OF GOD
in His
ECONOMY

WITNESS LEE

Living Stream Ministry
Anaheim, California

First Edition, February 1998.

ISBN 0-7363-0102-X

Published by

Living Stream Ministry
1853 W. Ball Road, Anaheim, CA 92804 U.S.A.
P. O. Box 2121, Anaheim, CA 92814 U.S.A.

Printed in the United States of America

98 99 00 01 02 03 / 9 8 7 6 5 4 3 2 1

CONTENTS

PREFACE

This book is a translation of messages given in Chinese by Brother Witness Lee in Anaheim, California on February 15-16, 1992. These messages were not reviewed by the speaker.

CHAPTER ONE

THE ECONOMY OF GOD AND
THE LAW OF GOD IN HIS ECONOMY

Scripture Reading: Eph. 1:10; 3:9; 1 Tim. 1:4b; Gen. 1:26-27;
2:9; Eph. 1:23; John 15:5a; Eph. 5:31-32; Gen. 2:18b; Phil.
1:20-21; Rom. 5:12, 19a, 20a; Exo. 32:15; Psa. 78:5; Exo.
20:3-17; Gal. 3:21; Rom. 8:3a; 3:20b; 5:20a; Gal. 3:23-24

OUTLINE

I. The economy of God—Eph. 1:10; 3:9; 1 Tim. 1:4b:
　A. To have man as His organism:
　　1. Having His image—Gen. 1:27.
　　2. Taking Him as life—Gen. 2:9.
　　3. Expressing Him.
　　4. Representing Him—Gen. 1:26.
　B. To be the Body of Christ—Eph. 1:23:
　　1. Being united and mingled with Christ—John
　　　15:5a:
　　　a. Having the same life and nature as Christ.
　　　b. Becoming one with Christ—Eph. 5:31-32.
　　2. As Christ's counterpart—cf. Gen. 2:18b:
　　　a. Living Christ—Phil. 1:21.
　　　b. Expressing Christ—the processed Triune
　　　　God—Phil. 1:20.
　C. The fall of man:
　　1. From God into sin—Rom. 5:12.
　　2. Man having been constituted a sinner in
　　　nature—Rom. 5:19a.
II. The law of God in His economy—Rom. 5:20a:
　A. The law of God being a portrait and testimony of
　　God—Exo. 32:15; Psa. 78:5.

B. God considering His law as His requirement upon sinners:
  1. The first three commandments requiring man to have only God and not have any idols aside from God—Exo. 20:3-7.
  2. The fourth commandment requiring man to take only God and all that God has accomplished for man as man's satisfaction and rest—Exo. 20:8-11.
  3. The fifth commandment requiring man to honor his parents and trace back to his source, his origin—the God who created man—Exo. 20:12.
  4. The sixth through the tenth commandments requiring man to live out the virtues that express God according to God's attributes—Exo. 20:13-17.
C. It being impossible for sinners to fulfill the requirements of God's law:
  1. The law of God not being able to give life—Gal. 3:21.
  2. There being something that the law of God could not do in that it was weak through the flesh of sinners—Rom. 8:3a.
D. The law of God being able only to expose man's sinful nature and wicked deeds—Rom. 3:20b; 5:20a.
E. The law of God becoming the custodian and child-conductor of God's chosen people to bring them to Christ—grace—Gal. 3:23-24.

The general subject of this Chinese New Year's conference is the law and grace of God in His economy. We are not here merely to see the law and grace of God; it is not that simple. What we want to see is the law and grace of God in His economy. We will cover this general subject with four messages. The contents of this general subject are:

1) God's economy is to work out an organism for His Divine Trinity.

2) The law in God's economy is used by God to expose the sinner's sinful nature and wicked deeds.

3) The grace in God's economy as the embodiment of God is to be received by man as man's enjoyment and supply.

4) The accomplishment of the experience of the grace in God's economy is the organic Body of Christ, which consummates in the New Jerusalem.

God's economy, the law of God in His economy, and the grace of God in His economy—these three things—are the subject of the entire Bible. From the first chapter of Genesis to the last chapter of Revelation, what is the entire Bible with sixty-six books concerned with? Some say that the Bible is a book on ethics and morality that tells husbands to love their wives and wives to be subject to their own husbands. Others say that the Bible is an excellent book of literature that contains many proverbs with admonitions. Still others say that the Bible is a book on science, since more than 2,700 years ago, at the time Isaiah wrote his book, he said that God sits above the circle of the earth, indicating that he already knew that the earth was round. Furthermore, there are others who say that the Bible is a book of prophecies, for it refers to the seventy weeks, which cover the entire human history and the end of the world. Although the Bible speaks of all these things, these matters are not its central subject. What is its central subject? The central subject of the Bible is God's economy.

I. THE ECONOMY OF GOD

Now we would like to see the economy of God, which is a very great subject. Ephesians 1:10, 3:9, and 1 Timothy 1:4 are three portions of the Word that are focused on God's economy.

God's economy came out of His heart's desire, which is His delight. The eternal God, the infinite God, surely has His heart's desire. The desire of God's heart is God's good pleasure. For the sake of His heart's desire and His good pleasure, God designed a plan in eternity to accomplish His purpose that He might obtain His heart's delight, His heart's desire, and His good pleasure. This plan, this design, is God's economy.

A. To Have Man as His Organism

According to the book of Ephesians, God's economy is to obtain an organism. God is infinite and intangible, yet He desires to gain the tangible man that He might enter into man to be man's life organically. God is concealed and invisible, yet He desires to be united and mingled with the tangible man that He may have a visible, tangible expression. This expression is not an expression of man but an expression of God, who dwells in man as man's life.

Take for example a lectern. A lectern is an object with a form and an appearance, yet it is inorganic because there is no life in it. In contrast, I am a living person. I am not merely an object with a form and an appearance; I have something intangible within me that is called life. Because I have life within me, there is something organic in me; therefore, my whole being is an organism. God's intention is to gain man as His organism, an organism that bears His image (Gen. 1:27) and takes Him as life (2:9) to express Him and represent Him (1:26) so that He may glorify Himself, that is, express Himself in glory. Furthermore, this expression is not something invisible or abstract; it is something visible and tangible within a body. This body is not God's own image and form; it is the image and form of a God-man as the issue of the union and mingling of God with man—God being expressed through the human form. Such a body is not only the uniting together of God and man but the union of God with man as one that all God's glory may be manifested through the human form.

B. To Be the Body of Christ

God's intention is for such an organism to be the Body of

Christ (Eph. 1:23) that this organism may be united and min- gled with Christ (John 15:5a) and have the same life and nature as Christ, that the two may become one (Eph. 5:31-32) as Christ's counterpart (cf. Gen. 2:18b) to live Christ (Phil. 1:21) and express Christ as the processed Triune God (v. 20).

The first step God took for the accomplishment of such an economy was creation. His old creation was with man as its center. He finished the creation of all things in their great diversity within six days. When everything was complete, He created man. God created man in His inward image and according to His outward likeness so that man may be like God within and without. Man, however, could not be God Himself. This may be compared to a picture of you. It is you no matter from which angle we look at it, yet it is not you. Although it is your picture, you must admit that it is not you but just a picture of you. Your picture bears your image, your form, and your likeness, but you are not in it and it does not have you as its life. Hence, a picture is not organic; it is not an organism.

God created man in His inward image and according to His outward likeness that man may look like Him and repre- sent Him. However, man did not have God within him. Man only had the God-created life; man did not have the uncreated life of God. The created man was man but not God; he had the human nature but not the divine nature. He had God's form, image, and likeness but not God's life and nature; he surely was not God. For man to be God's organism and become the Body of Christ, man had to receive God as life. Therefore, God put man in front of the tree of life. This means that He intended for man to eat the fruit of the tree of life that man may receive Him as life.

C. The Fall of Man

Next to the tree of life was the tree of the knowledge of good and evil. God put man in front of the two trees and let man choose which tree he would eat. If man would make the right choice and would eat the right thing, he would be blessed and have life. If he would choose wrongly and eat wrongly, he would die. Today we still have these two choices.

Every time we choose rightly by eating the tree of life, we have life. Every time we choose wrongly by eating the tree of the knowledge of good and evil, we die. Today we Christians have this kind of experience daily. Adam, who was created by God, made the wrong choice between the tree of life and the tree of the knowledge of good and evil—he ate the fruit of the tree of the knowledge of good and evil. He did not eat of the tree of life, which signifies God as his life, that he might have God's life organically and live out God. He missed this opportunity because he ate the wrong thing. He ate of the tree of the knowledge of good and evil, which signifies Satan, who is the factor of death and in whom are all the elements of death. After eating of the tree of the knowledge of good and evil, Adam fell from God into sin (Rom. 5:12), and the substance of death entered into him to constitute him a sinner dead by nature (v. 19a). Adam not only committed a trespass and offended God and thus had an outward sinful act, but even more he had an inward sinful nature and was constituted a sinner. If someone does the wrong thing, it is easy to correct the problem. But if he eats the wrong thing, taking it into him, this is a matter relating to life; it becomes a matter of life and death. God's original intention was that man would be for the producing of an organism, but man altogether became sinful, falling under God's condemnation to suffer eternal perdition.

Since man had fallen into such a condition, what should God do? God still intends to accomplish His economy. He is the God with whom is the beginning and the end; He is the Alpha and the Omega. Once He starts something, He will never give it up. Therefore, He added the law in His economy.

II. THE LAW OF GOD IN HIS ECONOMY

Since man ate of the tree of the knowledge of good and evil, which signifies Satan, Satan's nature entered into man. This nature incites and stirs up man to endeavor to do good that he may please God. This becomes a vice of the fallen sinner. Some may be shocked upon hearing this, thinking that all religionists exhort and encourage people to do good, and they may wonder why I say that man's desire to do good is incited by Satan. Parents like to encourage their children to do good, and even you yourself have an inner desire to do good. Is it good or bad to determine to do good and to encourage others to do good? From man's standpoint, it is good. Today's society everywhere encourages people to do good. As far as human society is concerned, this is good, but as far as the accomplishing of God's economy is concerned, this is not good and is something against God.

God's intention in His economy is to accomplish a goal, that is, for the Divine Trinity to gain man to be His organism. God's economy is not to work out man's goodness; to work out man's goodness is something of God's enemy. Human goodness is God's enemy. What God wants is to have an organism that lives out God to express God, manifest God, and be joined with God as one. Such a living organism is what God wants. From the viewpoint of God's economy, for man to do good is for man to be in enmity with God.

Before the law was given, God first gave man a sweet promise; He promised the fallen sinner that the seed of woman would come. This seed of woman would destroy the enemy, the serpent, who had damaged man. The seed of woman would become man's righteousness and man's salvation. Prior to His coming, however, man would neither believe nor receive Him. Therefore, God had to decree His law to man. The law was not there in the origination of God's economy. It was added because of man's transgressions, while God's economy was proceeding (Gal. 3:19). Due to man's fall and his not knowing himself, God was forced to insert, to add, the law. To add implies that something was not there originally. The law was not there originally but was added later in order to expose man's real condition and true nature and thus show man the true picture of himself.

A. The Law of God
Being a Portrait and Testimony of God

The law of God is a portrait and testimony of God. In Romans 7 Paul says that the law is holy and spiritual and the commandment is holy, righteous, and good (vv. 12, 14). The law is good, holy, and spiritual, yet even so, it is only a portrait, a "photo," of God. The law describes to us what kind of God He is, what kind of image He bears, and what kind of attributes He possesses. Hence, the law as God's portrait is called "the testimony" of God in the Old Testament (Exo. 32:15; Psa. 78:5). God's portrait, God's description, is God's testimony. Your photo is your testimony. When you give me a picture of yourself, you testify to me what kind of person you are. The moment I look at the picture, I know what kind of person you are. Similarly, the law is a portrait and testimony of God. When we see the law of God, we know what kind of God He is.

B. God Considering His Law
as His Requirement upon Sinners

1. The First Three Commandments Requiring Man
to Have Only God and Not Have
Any Idols aside from God

God considers His law as His requirement upon sinners. The contents of the law mainly are the Ten Commandments. The first three commandments require us to have only God and not have any idols aside from God (Exo. 20:3-7). They charge us repeatedly not to have graven images or other gods besides Jehovah, nor make images or worship them. In other words, we should have only God, and besides Him, we should not have any other object which we worship and by which we are occupied. If someone loves a pair of shoes, that pair of shoes is an idol on his feet. If someone loves his hairstyle, that hairstyle is an idol on his head. If someone loves having a Ph.D., that degree is the idol in his heart. Some people love their houses and possessions, others love their bank accounts, and still others love their reputation and position—all these things are idols. If you look from this angle, who among those living on earth today does not have idols? Everyone has idols, and there are not very many who want God. Very few are those who simply want nothing but God. Quite often I am afraid that if I like a certain thing, I might love that thing more than I love God. Many people shed tears today for various reasons, but I have rarely seen some brothers or sisters shed tears for the Lord. Almost all of those who have been close to me have shed tears in front of me, but who has shed tears for the Lord? I am afraid that you have not once shed tears for the Lord. You have shed tears before the Lord but not for Him; you wept because you did not graduate from college, because you failed to obtain a Ph.D., or because the promotion that you pursued went to another person. You should know that this kind of shedding of tears contradicts the first three commandments. You have violated God's law, you have desired other gods, and you have created idols.

2. The Fourth Commandment Requiring Man to Take Only God and All That God Has Accomplished for Man as Man's Satisfaction and Rest

The fourth commandment requires man to take only God and all that God has accomplished for man as man's satisfaction and rest (Exo. 20:8-11). This commandment concerns the keeping of the Sabbath. I read the Bible for several decades, but I did not quite understand why in His Ten Commandments God made such a commandment to set up a day and require man to keep it as the Sabbath. What is the meaning of this? Furthermore, when the Lord Jesus came, He did not want man to keep the Sabbath. Before the Lord Jesus came, God wanted man to keep the Sabbath. Then when the Lord Jesus came, although man still desired to keep the Sabbath, the Lord did not want man to keep it any longer. What does this mean?

It was not until these last six years that I began to understand what it means to keep the Sabbath. The keeping of the Sabbath means that you can take only God and all that He has done for you as your satisfaction, enjoyment, and rest. Keeping the Sabbath indicates that you have nothing on earth other than God; you take only God Himself and all that He has accomplished for you as your enjoyment, satisfaction, and rest. Your God is your everything, and He has accomplished everything for you. All you need to do is enjoy Him and take Him as your satisfaction and rest. Let me give you an illustration. I remember my old mother, who was a Christian. She loved her children very much and often cooked good food for us during holidays or on the Lord's Days. She had a peculiarity that while she loved to cook good meals for us, she had to do it all by herself and did not want us to do anything. If we would sit there and watch her doing everything and then praise her for doing such an excellent job, she would be very happy. If we would say, "Mother, you have been too busy; let me help you," she would be unhappy. She did not want us to help because she considered that an insult to her. Hence, we children knew that we just needed to wait for our mother to prepare the food for us and that we did not have to do anything. When the dumplings were done, we just praised her that her dumplings were really delicious; then she was very satisfied. While all of us were eating, she did not eat but just watched us and waited on us that we might have the enjoyment. When I was young, I could not understand her, but now that I look back, I realize that this is the way God deals with us. He is doing things for us, but if we try to help Him, the more we help, the more work He has to do. He does not want our help. Rather, He wants to do everything for us. Today everything is ready, and all we need to do is to come to the feast and enjoy Him. What does it mean to keep the Sabbath? To keep the Sabbath is to take God and everything that He has done for us as our satisfaction, enjoyment, and rest. Otherwise, we violate the Sabbath. When the Lord Jesus came, the Sabbath was simply the Lord, for the Lord is the real Sabbath. Therefore, there is no longer the need for us to keep the Sabbath as a ritual.

3. The Fifth Commandment Requiring Man to Honor His Parents and Trace Back to His Source, His Origin— the God Who Created Man

The fifth commandment requires us to honor our parents and thus trace back to our source, our origin—the God who created us (Exo. 20:12). I truly know that many Christians behave in a way that matches the experience of the Chinese people. People in northern China have a proverb: "No honoring, no befriending." This means that if a person does not honor his parents, you should not make friends with him. This is a sound word. However, almost no one knows what the ultimate meaning of honoring our parents is. To honor our parents is to remember our source. We came from our parents; without our parents, how could we have existence? But where did our parents come from? When we trace back to our source, our origin, we trace back to God. I believe that everyone who honors his parents venerates God. Hence, although it seems that the fifth commandment is concerned with parents and is therefore related to man, it is listed in the first group of five items, which belongs to the first tablet of stone, and is related to God.

4. The Sixth through the Tenth Commandments Requiring Man to Live Out the Virtues That Express God according to God's Attributes

The sixth through the tenth commandments require man to live out the virtues that express God according to God's attributes (Exo. 20:13-17). The second tablet of stone contained the latter five commandments, which are all related to man. The first of these commandments is not to kill, not to murder; the second is not to commit adultery, not to commit fornication; the third is not to steal, not to rob; the fourth is not to bear false witness against others, not to lie; and the fifth is not to covet, not to be greedy for others' possessions. If you violate any of these five commandments, you overthrow God's attributes and do not manifest God's virtues. What are God's attributes? They are love, light, holiness, and righteousness. God is love and full of kindness; God is light and full of brightness, without any darkness. God is holiness; He is transcendent, different from everything else, extraordinary, and distinct from all common things. God is righteousness; He is right, not crooked or biased, not twisted or distorted, but just, upright, and right in every way.

God is love, light, holiness, and righteousness, but what about us? Some say that they have never killed anyone and therefore have never violated the sixth commandment. However, when the Lord Jesus came, He gave a deeper word concerning killing. He said that to hate people is to kill people. Can you say that you have never hated others? Just consider a little: Among the people you have met, who does not hate others? To hate is to kill. Concerning adultery, the Lord Jesus also gave a deeper word. He said that every one who looks at a woman in order to lust after her has already committed adultery with her in his heart (Matt. 5:27-28). Concerning stealing, I have to confess publicly that before I was saved at the age of eighteen, I had stolen from others. May I ask whether or not you have you stolen anything? You may have taken the pencils from your company and used them at home. That was stealing. Any stealing or robbery is contrary to the virtues which are the manifestation of the divine attributes. Fourth, have you ever lied? We have lied too much. Not to speak of your entire life, if you did not lie only yesterday, you are almost an angel! The last commandment is concerned with covetousness. Who does not covet? When you see others riding in a luxurious car imported from Europe and you are riding in a Japanese-made car, you may begin to imagine in your heart that you will also ride in a European car one day. This is covetousness.

C. It Being Impossible for Sinners to Fulfill the Requirements of God's Law

The law, therefore, exposes our condition, showing us that it is impossible for sinners to fulfill the requirements of God's law. Although man cannot do good, he desires and wills to do good. Actually, man's condition is that he does not care for God; rather, he cares for things other than God. He does not take God as his satisfaction nor takes what God has accomplished as his enjoyment and rest; rather, he wants to strive by himself and bear the burdens alone. Today people have fallen into a condition of hatred, murder, and fornication. Today people commit fornication like those at the time of Sodom. Atheists greatly advocate evolution, and homosexuality is fornication to the uttermost. Evolution is atheism in its extreme, and homosexuality is human fornication in its extreme. I can tell you that most of those who believe in evolution do not honor their parents, and those who engage in homosexuality commit fornication to the uttermost.

Since man's condition is such, God considers His law, His reality, as His requirements upon sinners. It is as if He says to man who desires to do good, "These are My requirements. Do you want to do good? Go ahead! If you can work out all the Ten Commandments, I will justify you." According to Romans 7, it seems that Paul was able to work out the first nine commandments, but he was not able to work out the last commandment concerning not coveting. The law of God makes it impossible for sinners to fulfill the requirements of God, because God's law is for the purpose of exposing man. It cannot give life (Gal. 3:21). The law as a "photo" is good, but it does not have life. Furthermore, there is something that the law cannot do, in that it is weak through the flesh of sinners (Rom. 8:3a). The law itself is not weak, but the flesh of man that tries to work out the law is weak, so the law became weak and impotent.

D. The Law of God Being Able Only to Expose Man's Sinful Nature and Wicked Deeds

Since the law cannot give life and is impotent, being weak through the flesh of sinners, why did God add the law? The law of God was added for the purpose of exposing man's inward, sinful nature and his outward, wicked deeds (Rom. 3:20b; 5:20a). I have briefly presented the Ten Commandments with very simple illustrations. According to my presentation, you cannot escape. You have violated every one of the Ten Commandments. The law is a mirror. When we stand before the mirror of the law, we all are exposed.

E. The Law of God Becoming the Custodian and Child-conductor of God's Chosen People to Bring Them to Christ—Grace

Nevertheless, the law of God has a positive function in God's hand. The law has become the custodian and child-conductor of God's chosen people to bring them to Christ—grace (Gal. 3:23-24). God's chosen people were shut up and guarded under the law, just like sheep being kept in the sheepfold (John 10:1, 16). In His economy God used the law as a sheepfold to keep His elect in custody until Christ came. The law was able only to demand and condemn; it could not give life. There is no life in the law; there are only commandments. Life is in Christ. He is the life-giving Spirit (1 Cor. 15:45b), the only One who is able to give life. When we are under law, we are just like children, and we need the law to be the custodian and child-conductor watching over us. This kind of watching over is not with an evil intention; it is for our protection. Hence, this custodian becomes our child-conductor, and this child-conductor brings us to Christ. Today Christ as the life-giving Spirit is the grace that we enjoy. When Christ comes, grace comes. He became flesh and was full of grace, and of His fullness we have all received, and grace upon grace. Now we are no longer children under the custody of the law. Rather, through our faith in Christ Jesus we have become children of God to enjoy Him as our grace.

CHAPTER TWO

THE GRACE OF GOD IN HIS ECONOMY

Scripture Reading: Rom. 6:14; Heb. 8:13, 7, 6b; John 1:1, 14, 17b; 2 Cor. 8:9a; 13:14a; 1 Pet. 1:2b; 2 Pet. 1:2; Eph. 1:7b-8; Rom. 5:15b, 20b; Eph. 1:6-7; Rom. 3:24; 5:2a; John 1:16; 1 Tim. 1:14; Eph. 2:5-8; 2 Thes. 2:16; Heb. 4:16; 2 Cor. 9:8; Rev. 22:21; James 4:6; 1 Pet. 5:5; 2 Tim. 4:22; Luke 1:28, 30; Gal. 2:20-21; 2 Cor. 12:9; 8:1-2; 1 Pet. 5:10; Eph. 3:2, 8; 4:28-29; 1 Cor. 15:10; Rom. 5:17b, 21b; Acts 4:33; 11:23

OUTLINE

I. The New Testament believers being not under the law in God's economy but under the grace in God's economy—Rom. 6:14:

A. The law being for the old covenant in God's economy, which is also called the first covenant, a covenant which is becoming old and growing decrepit and which is near to disappearing—Heb. 8:13b, 7a.

B. Grace being for the new covenant in God's economy, which is also called the second covenant, the better covenant—Heb. 8:13a, 7c, 6b.

II. The grace of God in His economy being His embodiment:

A. God becoming flesh to be grace for man's enjoyment—John 1:1, 14.

B. Grace coming through Jesus Christ—the grace of Christ—John 1:17b; 2 Cor. 8:9a; 13:14a.

III. The grace of God in His economy being rich, multiplying, and abounding—Eph. 2:7; 1 Pet. 1:2b; 2 Pet. 1:2; Eph. 1:7b-8:

    A. The grace of God and the gift in grace of Jesus Christ having abounded to the many—Rom. 5:15b, 20b.

    B. Graced in Christ—Eph. 1:6.

    C. Through the redemption of Christ—Eph. 1:7; Rom. 3:24.

    D. By the believers' faith—Rom. 5:2a.

    E. Of His fullness the believers having all received, and grace upon grace—John 1:16.

IV. The believers' experience of the grace in God's economy:

    A. Having faith and love through the Lord's superabounding grace—1 Tim. 1:14.

    B. Receiving the salvation in life in Christ's resurrection and ascension—Eph. 2:5-8.

    C. Having obtained access into and standing in God's abounding grace—Rom. 5:2a.

    D. Enjoying eternal comfort and good hope in grace—2 Thes. 2:16.

    E. Coming forward with boldness to the throne of grace to find grace for timely help—Heb. 4:16.

    F. Receiving God's abounding supply of all grace—2 Cor. 9:8.

    G. Constantly enjoying God's multiplying grace—1 Pet. 1:2b; 2 Pet. 1:2; Rev. 22:21.

    H. Enjoying God's greater grace by being humble—James 4:6; 1 Pet. 5:5.

    I. Enjoying the Lord's presence in our spirit—2 Tim. 4:22; cf. Luke 1:28, 30.

    J. Living out God's righteousness by Christ—Gal. 2:20-21.

    K. Experiencing the perfecting of the Lord's sufficient grace, Christ's overshadowing power, in our weakness—2 Cor. 12:9.

    L. Displaying the riches of liberality in the depth of poverty—2 Cor. 8:1-2.

    M. Being perfected, established, strengthened, and grounded by God's all grace after having suffered—1 Pet. 5:10.

N. Carrying out the stewardship of the grace of God entrusted by Him—dispensing to people the riches of Christ as the grace of God—Eph. 3:2, 8.

O. In our living, speaking words for building up and thus giving grace to people—Eph. 4:28-29.

P. Being a surpassing one and laboring abundantly for the Lord—1 Cor. 15:10.

Q. Reigning in life by receiving the abundance of grace and of the gift of righteousness—grace reigning unto eternal life—Rom. 5:17b, 21b.

V. All believers having grace upon them and the church being built up:

  A. All believers having great grace upon them— Acts 4:33.

  B. The grace received by the believers being visible— Acts 11:23.

Thank the Lord! In these last days God is speaking among us. To be without God's speaking is a terrible thing. Without God's word, we would be in darkness; without God's word, we would cast off restraint; and without God's word, we would fall completely into death. If we have God's word, everything is all right. God's word is light, God's word is revelation, God's word is life, God's word is supply, and God's word is simply God Himself, the Lord Himself, and the Spirit Himself. In this message I hope that the Lord would grant us grace and give us His speaking that we may see what the grace of God in His economy is.

As Christians, we are very familiar with the term *grace,* and we have often come across it in our reading of the New Testament. John 1:14 says, "The Word became flesh and tabernacled among us...full of grace and reality." God became flesh and tabernacled among us, full of grace. This shows that grace is the incarnated God. If God remained in Himself, He could not become grace. If God was merely God and was not incarnated to become a man, He could not be grace. Hence, in the Old Testament the word "grace" is used very little, because at that time God had not become flesh and could not become grace. In the New Testament, however, God became flesh, and when He became flesh, He became grace.

In the previous message we saw the economy of God and the law of God in His economy. God's economy is to work out an organism for His Divine Trinity. No one knows how long God had been in eternity, and it is very difficult for anyone to know what He did in eternity past. According to my study of the Word, He did only one thing in eternity; that is, the Divine Trinity—the Father, the Son, and the Spirit—held a council. In that council the Triune God decided that the divine economy was to have an organism. We need the entire Bible to explain the contents of that counsel. What is covered from the first chapter of Genesis to the last chapter of Revelation is the content of that divine counsel in eternity. The content is that God created the heavens, the earth, and all things, and among all things He created the human race that the human race may have His image.

When I first read the Bible and came to the word *image,* I was puzzled. Does not the Bible tell us that God has no form or image? Then, how could God create man in His image and according to His likeness? Some say that God's image and likeness is man. In Genesis 18, before the Lord Jesus became flesh, He appeared with two angels in the form of man. That was God's outward likeness. He fellowshipped and had a conversation with Abraham, and Abraham gave Him water to wash His feet. Furthermore, Sarah, Abraham's wife, prepared a meal and brought it for Him to eat. Therefore, God's image and likeness is man. In the beginning I accepted such an explanation to a certain extent. However, the more I studied the Bible, the more I was bothered and the more I was not satisfied with such an explanation.

God indeed created man in His image and according to His likeness. Gradually I began to see that the image refers to what God is inwardly—His divine attributes. For example, God is love, God is light, God is holiness, and God is righteousness. These are the four great attributes of God. What God is, is love, light, holiness, and righteousness. Love and light are easy to understand. Holiness refers to God's being transcendent, different and distinct from all things; this is holiness. Righteousness refers to God's being absolutely right, not crooked or biased, not twisted or distorted, but perfect, just, upright, and right from any angle; this is righteousness. God is love, light, holiness, and righteousness. These are God's attributes. These attributes are inward; they are within God's being.

Likeness is how God appears outwardly. Image and likeness are not two things. The former is God's inward being, and the latter is the outward expression of God's inward being. The outward expression of God is His likeness. What is expressed outwardly is God's virtues. Attributes are inward, but when they are expressed, they become virtues. God is love; this is something within God. When God as love is expressed, that is God's virtue. God created man in His inward attributes and according to His outward virtues. Hence, man is very noble. Man is a photo of God's inward attributes and outward virtues. This is how God created man.

Praise the Lord! Among all the creatures, man is the only one who expresses God's attributes and God's virtues. Man bears God's inward image and God's outward likeness. Although man was created in such an excellent way, God did not put Himself into man. Man did not have God's life, God's nature, or God Himself within him. You may take a very good picture of me, but after seeing it, I would say, "This picture is good, but it is not good enough because I am not really in the picture. That picture does not have my life, my nature, or myself."

This is how God created Adam in the beginning. Adam had God's image and God's likeness but not God's life, God's nature, or God Himself. A picture of you cannot fully express you; it can only give others a general idea of your form. Regardless how good the picture of a person is, it cannot fully express the person himself. A photo is dead; it is lifeless. I, however, am full of life; my entire being is organic. No picture can express me organically. After he was created, Adam had God's image and God's likeness. He had both God's inward being and outward expression, but he did not have God's life or nature. This means that he did not have God Himself. Since he did not have God as his person, he could neither represent God nor express God. Hence, he could not achieve the purpose of becoming God's organism. He was not qualified to be God's organism because neither his image nor his likeness was organic; he did not have God as his life.

In His economy God did not intend to have merely a "photo." Rather, God's intention was that the man whom He created would become His organism to express Him. Therefore, God put Adam into a garden. In the garden there were many trees, and in the middle there was the tree of life. There was also another tree, the tree of the knowledge of good and evil. The tree of life gives life to man, and the tree of the knowledge of good and evil brings death to man. One of these two trees signifies God as the source of life, and the other signifies Satan as the element of death. The Bible calls Satan the one "who has the might of death" (Heb. 2:14). Everything that is of death is stored up and accumulated in Satan. God is the source of life; Satan is the hotbed of death.

After the creation of man, God brought man in front of the two trees and warned him, "Of every tree of the garden thou mayest freely eat: but of the tree of the knowledge of good and evil, thou shalt not eat of it: for in the day that thou eatest thereof thou shalt surely die" (Gen. 2:16-17). Instead of eating of the tree of life, Adam ate of the tree of the knowledge of good and evil. Originally, Adam was the good material that could receive the tree of life. This means that he could receive God into him as his life and nature, that is, as his person. However, after Adam ate of the tree of the knowledge of good and evil, Satan's life and nature, even Satan himself, entered into him. Adam's transgression was not only due to his wrongdoing outwardly but due to his eating something wrong inwardly. This resulted in his being constituted a sinner in his nature.

The counsel that God made in the council in eternity was only half-accomplished when Satan interrupted it. Satan put his sinful nature into man so that it became man's sinful nature. Thus, man was constituted a sinner and was condemned before God unto perdition. Hence, in Genesis 3, after the fall of man, God came to proclaim the glad tidings. Adam and Eve hid themselves from God's presence because they were afraid of God. Furthermore, they had made themselves aprons of leaves to cover the shame of their nakedness. At that time, God came and called to Adam, saying, "Where art thou?" Then He said to the serpent, "I will put enmity between thee and the woman, / and between thy seed and her seed; / it shall bruise thy head, / and thou shalt bruise his heel" (vv. 9, 15). This was a promise. Not only so, but after speaking such a word, God killed a lamb and used its skin to make coats for Adam and Eve. It seems that God was saying to Adam, "Don't make aprons of leaves for yourself. The aprons of leaves are your own labor, and they cannot give you rest. Put on My coats!" As soon as they put on the coats, they had rest. This was the gospel, which was a gospel of promise: The seed of woman would come. When He came, on the one hand, He bruised the head of the serpent, and on the other hand, He was killed, shedding His blood for our sins and thus becoming righteousness to us, the sinners, that we may be justified and delivered from the devil.

After God gave such a promise, not much seemed to happen. According to the record of the Bible, it seems that God did not do much, except to tell Adam and his descendants that over and over they had to kill bulls and goats as sacrifices to cover their sins. Two thousand years passed from Adam to Abraham. During that period, man fell from God into sin; this means that he fell from God's ruling into the ruling of his own conscience. After another fall, man fell from the ruling of conscience into the ruling of human government. Eventually, in Noah's time, God came in to execute His judgment by destroying the people of that generation with the flood. After Noah, man fell again and again until eventually he fell into Babel. At Babel man was altogether in rebellion against God and in the worship of idols. Therefore, out of that place—Babel—God chose a man and called him. That man was Abram, whose name was later changed to Abraham. God brought him to the land of Canaan and told him that He would give that land to him and to his seed, and that in his seed all the families of the earth would be blessed (Gen. 12:3). This gospel was much greater than the gospel in Genesis 3. However, we have to know that the seed of woman in Genesis 3 is the seed of Abraham in Genesis 12. The seed of woman who would bruise the serpent's head is the seed of Abraham in whom all the families of the earth would be blessed. Abraham did not merely receive a promise as Adam did. God swore to Abraham and made a covenant with him. That covenant made with an oath was the predecessor of the new covenant.

The predecessor of the new covenant was the covenant God made with Abraham based on the promise He gave to Adam. In this covenant God promised that Abraham would beget a son, a seed, in whom the families of the earth would be blessed. In Galatians 3 Paul says that today we who have believed in the Lord Jesus have received the blessing which God promised to Abraham with a covenant, that is, the promise of the Spirit (v. 14). The Spirit is also called the Spirit of grace. When the blessing that God gave to Abraham comes to us, it is grace; this grace is the seed of Abraham, which is also the seed of woman.

It was two thousand years from Adam to Abraham and another two thousand years from Abraham to Christ. It took four thousand years for God's promise to Adam to be fulfilled. With God, however, there is no element of time; in God's eyes, one thousand years are like one day. In those two thousand years from Abraham to Christ, it seems again that God did not do anything. During that period, the descendants of Abraham went down to Egypt and were under the slavery of Pharaoh for four hundred thirty years. At the fullness of those four hundred thirty years, God came in again to lead them out of Egypt. However, after leading them out, God did not bring them immediately into Canaan. Thus, the children of Israel wandered in the wilderness for forty years.

After the passing of forty years, the aged Moses was already one hundred twenty years old. He reiterated God's law and encouraged the children of Israel to enter Canaan. Then, after their entrance into Canaan, it was not until approximately five hundred years had elapsed, at the time of David, that they subdued all the enemies within their borders. Eventually, Solomon, the son of David, built the temple for God. Unfortunately, this wonderful situation did not last long. Solomon was excellent in the beginning but became corrupt in his old age. He indulged in lusts and selected a thousand wives and concubines for himself. Many among these wives were heathen women who brought in heathen gods. He was corrupted and so were his descendants. Eventually, the Jewish people were defeated first by Assyria and later by Babylon and Medo-Persia. Sixty years before Christ's birth, the Roman Empire conquered the king of the Jews and thus brought in the fall of the Jewish nation.

The children of Israel were under such circumstances for two thousand years, but eventually Christ was born. He was the seed of woman, the seed of Abraham, and the seed of David. He was God who became flesh and was born in a manger. Later He was taken to Egypt to escape Herod's slaying. Hence, not only the children of Israel but even the Lord Jesus went down to Egypt. After His birth, He did not do anything but first went down to Egypt. This proves that the incarnated Savior was joined with His redeemed as one. He went down to Egypt just as His redeemed did. Then one day God called His Son out of Egypt, and this Son is a corporate Son, who includes Israel as well as Christ. This Son came out of Egypt and returned to Nazareth, where He grew up until the full age of thirty when He came out to minister. After three and a half years, He was crucified. On the night when He was going to die, He established a new covenant with His disciples (Luke 22:20). That new covenant was the new covenant spoken of in Jeremiah 31 as the continuation of the covenant that God made with Abraham.

I. THE NEW TESTAMENT BELIEVERS BEING NOT UNDER THE LAW IN GOD'S ECONOMY BUT UNDER THE GRACE IN GOD'S ECONOMY

The New Testament believers are not under the law in God's economy but under the grace in God's economy (Rom. 6:14). Today we are not the saints in the Old Testament who were under the law; rather, as the New Testament believers, we are all under the grace of God.

A. The Law Being for the Old Covenant in God's Economy, Which Is Also Called the First Covenant, a Covenant Which Is Becoming Old and Growing Decrepit and Which Is Near to Disappearing

To carry out God's economy and achieve the purpose of obtaining an organism for God involves two covenants. One covenant is a covenant that existed originally, and the other covenant is a covenant added along the way, a covenant that should have been unnecessary. The Bible uses two women to signify these two covenants: The first woman is Sarah, the wife of Abraham as the rightful woman, and the other woman is Hagar, who was a concubine. In the Bible, the position of the law is like that of a concubine and not like that of a rightful woman, so the children brought forth by the law were unto slavery and could not be reckoned as the free children of God (cf. Gal. 4:22-31).

In between the covenant that God made with Abraham

and the new covenant that the Lord enacted with His precious blood, there was the covenant of Moses. Moses, who, on the one hand, represented God, and on the other hand, represented Israel, enacted a covenant for the two parties, which covenant was the old covenant. The old covenant, referred to as "the first" in Hebrews 8, was a covenant which was becoming old and growing decrepit and which was near to disappearing (vv. 13b, 7a). This first covenant was a covenant that should not have existed; it was not in God's plan but was added along the way. We may illustrate this in the following way: A person drives from Anaheim to the airport, and because he has no plan to see a doctor on the way, he expects to arrive at the airport in fifty minutes. However, along the way he has an accident and is injured. The car is pulled aside, while a policeman calls a doctor. This is the story of the law of the Old Testament. According to Romans 5, the law was something added; it was not something in the original plan but was inserted afterwards. The law is God's portrait, God's photograph; it is not God Himself. The photograph came first, and then the person Himself followed. The law is God's photograph, and grace is God Himself. Before God came, He first sent a picture to testify of Himself and also to expose man's real condition. God knew that man had fallen to such an extent that he was filled with the devil, having the devil's life and nature and even the devil himself, so that man could not walk according to God's law.

B. Grace Being for the New Covenant
in God's Economy, Which Is Also Called
the Second Covenant, the Better Covenant

When the Lord Jesus came (by God's incarnation), grace came. Grace is for the new covenant in God's economy, which is also called the second covenant, the better covenant (Heb. 8:13a, 7c, 6b). The law requires us to do something by ourselves; grace is God doing something for us. Actually, we do not have to do anything, and we cannot do anything. God does not require us to do anything; He does everything for us from the beginning to the end. It was God who carried out His incarnation, it was He who lived out His human living for thirty-three and a half years, it was He who accomplished the all-inclusive death on the cross, it was He who attained His entrance into resurrection, and it was He who accomplished His entrance into ascension. Everything was accomplished by Him. We just need to enter into His accomplishments and enjoy Him as our rest. This is grace.

II. THE GRACE OF GOD IN HIS ECONOMY BEING HIS EMBODIMENT

A. God Becoming Flesh to Be Grace for Man's Enjoyment

The grace of God in His economy is His embodiment. God became flesh that He may enter into man and be mingled with man as one; this is Emmanuel. He is the God-man; He is God yet man, and man yet God. God and man became one in Him. This Emmanuel, the incarnated God, is grace for man's enjoyment (John 1:1, 14). Here we have One who was God becoming man, who was called Emmanuel and who was also called Jesus. He is grace. I hope that we all can see this revelation and vision. What is grace? Grace is the embodied God. First, God as the Father was embodied in the Son, and then the Son was realized as the life-giving Spirit. This Spirit enters into us as grace for our enjoyment.

We must see what grace is. Grace is the embodiment of God, who became a God-man with divinity and humanity, passed through human living, died, resurrected, and entered into ascension. Now He has become the life-giving Spirit and is dwelling in us today. Therefore, 2 Timothy 4:22 says, "The Lord be with your spirit," and then it says, "Grace be with you." The Lord being with our spirit equals grace being with us. The Lord as grace is for us to receive and enjoy as our supply and experience.

B. Grace Coming through Jesus Christ— the Grace of Christ

This grace came through Jesus Christ; hence, it is the grace of Christ (John 1:17b; 2 Cor. 8:9a; 13:14a). In Greek, expressions such as *the grace of Christ* and *the love of God* are appositions. Grace and Christ, Christ and grace—the two are one. *The grace of Christ* does not mean that Christ is Christ and grace is grace; rather, it means that Christ is grace. Likewise, *the love of God* does not mean that outside of God there is something called love; rather, it means that God is love. This is the sense in 2 Corinthians 13:14, where the love of God, the grace of Christ, and the fellowship of the Holy Spirit are mentioned. God is love, Christ is grace, and the Holy Spirit is fellowship.

The first three stanzas of *Hymns*, #497 read as follows:

Grace in its highest definition is
God in the Son to be enjoyed by us;
It is not only something done or giv'n,
But God Himself, our portion glorious.

God is incarnate in the flesh that we
Him may receive, experience ourself;
This is the grace which we receive of God,
Which comes thru Christ and which is Christ Himself.

Paul the Apostle counted all as dung,
'Twas only God in Christ he counted grace;
'Tis by this grace—the Lord experienced—
That he surpassed the others in the race.

Grace to the apostle Paul was God in Christ. Can we also say that grace to us is God in Christ? I hope that we all can see that grace to us is God in Christ. All other things are not grace: neither wives nor husbands, neither sons nor daughters, neither properties nor bank accounts, neither education nor position. All these are not grace to us. Only God in Christ is grace to us. If we lose this Christ, we lose everything of grace. If we gain this Christ, He is everything of grace.

I hope that we all can see this matter. God has no intention to put us under the law; His intention is to put us in His grace. Today we are those who have received grace, which is the Triune God, which is the Father given to us in the Son, and which is the Son realized as the Spirit dwelling in our spirit. The Spirit dwelling in us is the practical grace. This is grace; we live this and we live by this. Apart from this, we can do nothing and we have nothing.

III. THE GRACE OF GOD IN HIS ECONOMY
BEING RICH, MULTIPLYING, AND ABOUNDING

A. The Grace of God and
the Gift in Grace of Jesus Christ
Having Abounded to the Many

The grace of God in His economy is rich, multiplying, and abounding (Eph. 2:7; 1 Pet. 1:2b; 2 Pet. 1:2; Eph. 1:7b-8). The riches of God's grace surpass every limitation. These are the riches of God Himself for our enjoyment. Furthermore, the grace of God and the gift in grace of Jesus Christ have abounded to the many (Rom. 5:15b, 20b).

B. Graced in Christ

God has graced us in Christ with the grace in His economy (Eph. 1:6). *Graced* here as a verb indicates that we have been put in the position of grace that we may become the object of God's grace and favor, that is, that we may enjoy all that God is to us.

C. Through the Redemption of Christ

A part of the grace of God in His economy is that Christ has become our redemption for the forgiveness of our offenses (Eph. 1:7). Moreover, we have been justified freely by the grace of God through the redemption which is in Christ Jesus (Rom. 3:24). It is through the redemption of Christ that we can enjoy this Christ who is grace.

D. By the Believers' Faith

On the one hand, we can enjoy Christ as grace through His redemption. On the other hand, we have obtained access by faith into this grace in which we stand (Rom. 5:2a). Faith issues in our justification, and it also gives us access into the grace of God. The Greek phrase for *believe into* has the sense of *entering into*. For example, there may be a jumbo jet here with everything ready, but we still must enter into the plane to enjoy flying. If we use our own flesh and its natural endeavor, we cannot enjoy God as grace, but if we believe into

Christ, we have access into the full enjoyment of the grace of God.

E. Of His Fullness the Believers
Having All Received, and Grace upon Grace

Finally, of His fullness the believers have all received, and grace upon grace (John 1:16). When Christ in us is daily received, enjoyed, and experienced by us, that is grace being added to us, grace upon grace.

IV. THE BELIEVERS' EXPERIENCE
OF THE GRACE IN GOD'S ECONOMY

A. Having Faith and Love
through the Lord's Superabounding Grace

Grace is Christ. All the spiritual experiences of a Christian should be experiences of Christ as grace. In our experience of the grace in God's economy, first, we have faith and love through the Lord's superabounding grace (1 Tim. 1:14). To be a believer is a matter of faith and love. Faith and love are products of the Lord's grace. Through faith we receive the Lord, and through love we enjoy the Lord whom we have received. We have neither faith nor love, but when we allow the Lord to come into us, both faith and love from the Lord as grace come into us.

When we preach the gospel, we infuse people with such a trustworthy and lovely Lord. I have been to Hong Kong numerous times, and I have noticed that the jewelers there have the skill of talking continually and unceasingly. If a jeweler is not able to convince you the first day, he will talk to you again the next day when you pass by his store. After listening, you cannot help but buy a piece of jewelry from him, because the jewelry is really lovable. However, if he showed you a lump of clay, regardless of what he said, you would never stop to listen to his talk. When we preach the gospel, we are presenting to people a treasure of peerless worth in the universe. After we finish our speaking, many will believe because what is good is simply good, and what is precious is simply precious. In the end, everyone will want what we speak of.

When the Lord as the One of peerless worth appears to us, we simply cannot run away from Him. The Lord is too wonderful. He is so beautiful and sweet; He is incomparable. I have read something concerning J. N. Darby, who was a teacher among the Brethren in the nineteenth century. He lived to be eighty years old and remained single his whole life. At the age of eighty, one day during his travels he was staying in a hotel alone. In his loneliness he had such a sweet feeling within that he knelt down and prayed, "O Lord Jesus, I still love You." This word touched me very much. Such a word coming from an old man proves how sweet the Lord Jesus is. What is this? This is the Lord Himself as grace coming into us to become our faith and love.

B. Receiving the Salvation in Life in Christ's Resurrection and Ascension

In their experience of the grace in God's economy, the believers also receive the salvation in life in Christ's resurrection and ascension (Eph. 2:5-8). This salvation is a salvation in life. We just need to believe into the Lord Jesus by calling on His name, confessing our sins, and praying to Him; then He will come into us. He is the resurrected and ascended One. Today He is in resurrection and ascension. When He comes into us, we are also resurrected and ascended in Him. This is salvation in life. This salvation is not something superficial; it is not merely to save us from hell. This salvation is the resurrected and ascended Lord. Today in His resurrection and ascension He has entered into us to be our person. We are also resurrected and seated in the heavenlies together with Him. This is the salvation that we have received. This salvation is the resurrected and ascended Christ becoming our grace.

C. Having Obtained Access into and Standing in God's Abounding Grace

The believers' experience of the grace in God's economy enables them to obtain access into and stand in God's grace (Rom. 5:2a). Today we are not under the law but under the grace in God's economy. This grace is God Himself. Sometimes I have heard people say that they flew from Taipei to

the United States. In my heart I said, "How could you fly
from Taipei? It is not you who flew but the airplane." Some
people say that they lean upon Jesus. This is wrong. If you fly
from Taipei to the United States by leaning upon the airplane, this leaning is not dependable. You do not lean upon
the airplane, but you enter into the airplane. You are resting
while the airplane is flying; you enjoy the restfulness of
flying. Noah was saved by entering into the ark, not by leaning upon the ark. Today we are standing in grace. This grace
is Christ, the pneumatic Christ, the life-giving Spirit.

D. Enjoying Eternal Comfort
and Good Hope in Grace

In this grace we enjoy God's eternal comfort and good hope
(2 Thes. 2:16). God's comfort is not temporary and transitory
comfort but eternal comfort. This eternal comfort is the eternal life. We have the eternal life in us, and this eternal life is
our eternal comfort. This comfort is sufficient for any kind of
environment and situation. Furthermore, we enjoy good hope
in grace. This means that at the Lord's coming, we will enter
into His glory.

E. Coming Forward with Boldness to the Throne
of Grace to Find Grace for Timely Help

Furthermore, in their experience of the grace in God's
economy, the believers come forward with boldness to the
throne of grace to find grace for timely help (Heb. 4:16). The
very Christ who is sitting on the throne in heaven is also now
in our spirit, where the habitation of God is (Eph. 2:22). Since
today our spirit is the place of God's habitation, when-
ever we turn to our spirit, we touch the throne in heaven, and
this throne is the throne of grace to us. When we come forward to the throne of grace, we receive Christ as grace for our
timely help.

F. Receiving God's Abounding Supply of All Grace

In their experience of the grace in God's economy, the
believers also receive God's abounding supply of all grace.
Second Corinthians 9:8 says, "God is able to make all grace

abound unto you, that, in everything always having all suffi-
ciency, you may abound unto every good work." Today we
have God abundantly supplying us with all grace.

G. Constantly Enjoying God's Multiplying Grace

We are constantly enjoying God's multiplying grace (1 Pet.
1:2b; 2 Pet. 1:2; Rev. 22:21). Peter spoke of this multiplying
grace in his first and second Epistles. This grace is not dead
but living and multiplying; it is being multiplied to us day by
day.

H. Enjoying God's Greater Grace by Being Humble

The believers also enjoy God's greater grace by being
humble (James 4:6; 1 Pet. 5:5). Grace has a measure. The
Lord Himself is without measure, but our experience of Him
has a measure. When we are humble and broad-minded, the
grace in us is greater. When we are proud and narrow-
minded, the grace in us is smaller. The measure of our enjoyment of God's grace depends on us. If we are broad, the grace
is greater; if we are narrow, the grace is smaller.

I. Enjoying the Lord's Presence in Our Spirit

In our experience of the grace in God's economy, we
enjoy the Lord's presence in our spirit (2 Tim. 4:22; cf. Luke
1:28, 30). The Lord being with us in our spirit is grace being
enjoyed by us in our spirit.

J. Living Out God's Righteousness by Christ

In their experience of the grace in God's economy, the
believers live out the righteousness of God by Christ (Gal.
2:20-21). Paul said that he did not live by his own righteousness but that he was crucified with Christ and it was Christ
who lived in him. Thus, what was lived out was the righteousness which God desired. If we do not live out God's
righteousness by Christ, we nullify the grace of God. If,
instead of nullifying the grace of God, we desire to enjoy it
daily, we need to live not by ourselves but by the Christ who
is in our spirit. Thus, what we live out is the righteousness
that God desires. This righteousness is of grace.

K. Experiencing the Perfecting of the Lord's Sufficient Grace, Christ's Overshadowing Power, in Our Weakness

The believers' experience of the grace in God's economy is the experience of the perfecting of the Lord's sufficient grace, Christ's overshadowing power, in our weakness (2 Cor. 12:9). Why is the Lord's grace perfected in our weakness? Because when a person is weak and cannot do anything, the Lord comes to do everything for him. When someone is strong, he does not need others. Would you rather be strong or weak? The good thing about being weak is that the Lord comes to do everything for you. The bad thing about being strong is that you put the Lord aside. When you are strong, the Lord has no ground and cannot do anything for you; hence, you cannot enjoy rest. When you are weak, the Lord has the ground and can do things for you right away. When the Lord does everything for you, you enjoy the Lord as your rest.

L. Displaying the Riches of Liberality in the Depth of Poverty

In their experience of the grace in God's economy, the believers display the riches of liberality in the depth of poverty (2 Cor. 8:1-2). This is the grace given by the Lord to the believers and the churches in Macedonia. This grace is Christ's resurrection life by which we overcome the usurpation of temporal and uncertain riches and become generous in ministering to the needy saints.

M. Being Perfected, Established, Strengthened, and Grounded by God's All Grace after Having Suffered

Our experience of the grace in God's economy is that after we have suffered, we are perfected, established, strengthened, and grounded by God's all grace (1 Pet. 5:10).

N. Carrying Out the Stewardship of the Grace of God Entrusted by Him—Dispensing to People the Riches of Christ as the Grace of God

In our experience of the grace in God's economy, we carry

out the stewardship of the grace of God entrusted by Him—dispensing the riches of Christ as the grace of God to His chosen people for the producing and building up of the church (Eph. 3:2, 8).

O. In Our Living, Speaking Words for Building Up and Thus Giving Grace to People

Not only the apostles as stewards dispensed grace into people, but we also, in our living, should speak words for building up and thus give grace to people. Ephesians 4:29 says, "Let no corrupt word proceed out of your mouth, but only that which is good for building up, according to the need, that it may give grace to those who hear." In verse 28 Paul said that we should labor, working with our own hands in that which is respectable, that we may have something to share with him who has need. As Christians, we should have something in our living, both materially and spiritually, to minister to others.

P. Being a Surpassing One and Laboring Abundantly for the Lord

Paul experienced the Lord's grace to be a surpassing one and to labor abundantly for the Lord (1 Cor. 15:10). The Lord whom he experienced enabled him to labor more abundantly than all the saints. When he did that, he experienced Christ as his grace. Today, the resurrected Christ brings the processed Triune God in resurrection into us to be our life and life supply that we may experience Him as grace and thus be a surpassing one and labor abundantly for the Lord.

Q. Reigning in Life by Receiving the Abundance of Grace and of the Gift of Righteousness— Grace Reigning unto Eternal Life

We reign in life by receiving the abundance of grace and of the gift of righteousness. This is grace reigning in life unto eternal life (Rom. 5:17b, 21b). The life we have received does not merely save us from a few things; rather, it enthrones us as kings to reign over all things. We have received righteousness objectively, but we still need to continually receive the abundance of grace so that we can reign in life subjectively. If we have the experience of the aforementioned sixteen items, we are those who stand in the abundance of grace. Then we can reign in life so that everything is controlled by us instead of everything directing us. This is to overcome. This is grace reigning unto eternal life.

V. ALL BELIEVERS HAVING GRACE UPON THEM AND THE CHURCH BEING BUILT UP

In the church life, when all the believers have grace upon them, the church will be built up. However, it is easy for us to come out of grace and argue with others. A person who has seen grace knows Christ and has nothing to argue about with others. If a person argues, he does not know grace. How do we stand in grace? Practically, it means that we come back to our spirit. We need to exercise to turn back to our spirit. When we return to our spirit, we stand in grace. Regardless of how much others criticize you, judge you, or dispute with you, never open your mouth and never reason. Instead, learn to return to your spirit. Once you begin to reason, you will begin to debate; if you keep arguing, you will end up murmuring. Do not reason or murmur; do not stay in your mind or in your emotion but be in spirit. When you are in spirit, you are in Christ; that is to stand in grace. Sometimes when you pray-read a verse or sing a hymn, the Lord's word will bring you into the grace in Christ. You may be full of reasonings and murmurings, but when you turn back to your spirit, you stand in grace. As a result, what comes out of your mouth is grace. In His economy God does not require you to do anything. What God wants in His economy is for Christ, the embodiment of the Triune God, to become the embodied grace to you. He lives in us, and we live in Him as grace. In this way God can obtain His organism.

A. All Believers Having Great Grace upon Them

Today we are not merely individual Christians, because it is not just one individual alone who receives grace, but all the believers receive great grace (Acts 4:33). No individual by himself is the organism of God. This organism is corporate, not individual. We have been crucified with Christ; now Christ is in us not only to be our life and life supply but also to be our person. Christ and we live together; two lives have one living, two natures are mingled into one nature, and two spirits become one spirit. Such a living is the organism for the processed and consummated Triune God to live among us organically for His expression. This is God's intention in His economy.

B. The Grace Received
by the Believers Being Visible

In such an organic church life, the grace received by the believers is visible (Acts 11:23). The Triune God received and enjoyed by the believers is expressed in their salvation, change in life, holy living, and the gifts they exercise in their meetings, all of which can be seen by others.

What God wants today is that we experience the grace in His economy so that the Divine Trinity may have an organism. Today people only talk about the universal church and the local churches; they debate a great deal, yet there is no manifestation of this organism. This is my concern. We may be right concerning the church both universally and locally, yet there may be no organism. This organism is not a matter of arguing about the local churches or the universal church; this organism depends on our going to the cross and on the resurrected Christ's being in us. We become one with Him as the One who died, resurrected, and ascended—two lives share one living, two natures are mingled into one nature (without producing a third nature), and two spirits become one spirit. If there is a group of brothers and sisters who live on the earth in this way, this group of brothers and sisters is the organism that God desires to have.

Brothers and sisters, if we study each of the items mentioned above, we will see that the apostles' teaching in the beginning was according to the pattern of their living. What they taught was concerning such an organism. They did not speak about the universal church or the local churches. If we only speak about these things, we are still speaking about the "photo"; we do not have God as the organic One in us. If we can see this and live in this organic One, instead of engaging in outward discussions and debates about the photo, we will experience great deliverance. Today the processed and consummated Triune God has become the life-giving Spirit and is all-inclusive. As such a One, He is in us to bring us all into His organism. In this organism is the organic element that God wants. It is not the outward explanation of doctrines. The more we are right in doctrine, the less organic element we have. The more we remain in the "photo," the less we are in the living person. I hope that our eyes will be opened to see where our real need is. We need to be in the processed and consummated Triune God, taking Him as our life and our person. We are on the cross, and yet in His resurrection we have been resurrected, and we have ascended with Him. Here, God and man are mingled to produce an organism. This is accomplished by grace. The grace in God's economy is the embodiment of God for man to receive as his enjoyment and supply. We should learn to receive such an embodied grace that we may have this enjoyment and supply. As a result, we will be full of the organic element in our inner being and thus become the organism of God.

CHAPTER THREE

THE GRACE IN GOD'S ECONOMY
IN THE BELIEVERS' EXPERIENCE

Scripture Reading: John 1:1, 14, 16-17; Matt. 28:19; John 14:8-11, 16-20; 7:37-39; 6:63; 20:22; 1 John 4:13; 2:27; Rev. 2:1, 7; 22:17, 21; Eph. 4:6; 2 Cor. 13:14; John 15:5; Eph. 3:17; Rom. 8:11, 16; 1 Cor. 15:45b; 2 Cor. 3:17; Heb. 10:29; Zech. 12:10; Rom. 8:4b-6; Rev. 22:1

OUTLINE

I. The grace in God's economy in the believers' experience being the processed Triune God:

A. God, who was in the beginning, becoming flesh in time as grace for man to receive, possess, and enjoy—John 1:1, 14, 16-17:

1. The incarnated God being triune—the Father, the Son, and the Spirit—Matt. 28:19:

a. The Father as the source being embodied and expressed in the Son—John 14:8-11.

b. The Son being realized as the Spirit and abiding in the believers—John 14:16-20.

c. The Spirit being in the believers as their life and life supply—the living water of life, the bread of life, and the breath of life—and becoming the divine grace enjoyed by them—John 7:37-39; 6:63; 20:22.

d. The indwelling Spirit, the processed Triune God, abiding in the believers as the anointing and becoming their enjoyment in life—1 John 4:13; 2:27.

  e. The anointing Spirit, the pneumatic Christ,
     the Spirit who speaks to the churches, even-
     tually becoming the counterpart of the
     church, the bride—Rev. 2:1, 7; 22:17.
  2. Such a processed and consummated Triune
     God being the grace enjoyed by all the believers
     in God's New Testament economy, even for eter-
     nity—Rev. 22:21.
  B. With the love, the grace, and the fellowship of the
     Divine Trinity as factors:
     1. With the love of God the Father, who is over all
        and through all and in all, as the source—Eph.
        4:6; 2 Cor. 13:14b.
     2. With the grace of God the Son, who abides in
        the believers and makes His home in their
        hearts, as the element—John 15:5; Eph. 3:17;
        2 Cor. 13:14a.
     3. With the fellowship of God the Spirit, who
        dwells in the believers and is mingled with
        their spirit as one spirit, as the distribu-
        tion—Rom. 8:11, 16; 2 Cor. 13:14b.
II. The New Testament believers' living under the grace
    in God's economy being a total living of experiencing
    the processed Triune God as grace:
  A. The processed Triune God, consummated as the
     all-inclusive, life-giving, compound, and indwell-
     ing Spirit, becoming the Spirit of grace—1 Cor.
     15:45b; 2 Cor. 3:17; Rev. 22:17a; Heb. 10:29:
     1. In the New Testament age the Spirit of grace
        dispensing the Triune God into the believers as
        grace.
     2. At the end of the New Testament age the Spirit
        of grace causing the whole house of Israel to
        repent and receive the Triune God as grace—
        Zech. 12:10.
  B. The compound, life-giving Spirit and the believers'
     regenerated spirit becoming one mingled spirit—
     Rom. 8:4b-6.
  C. The believers' living and work by the Spirit,

essentially and economically, being their experience and enjoyment of the pneumatic Christ, the
embodiment of the Triune God, as grace—John
1:14, 16; Rev. 22:21.

In this message we come to the most crucial point, which
is the grace in God's economy in the believers' experience. The
everyday experience of the believers must be grace. If it is not
grace, it is not the believers' experience; if it is not grace, it is
not the Christian living. The Christian living must be the
living of grace, the experience of grace. In the preceding message we saw that grace is God's embodiment—Christ. Hence,
the grace experienced by the believers is Christ, the embodiment of God.

I. THE GRACE IN GOD'S ECONOMY
IN THE BELIEVERS' EXPERIENCE BEING
THE PROCESSED TRIUNE GOD

The grace in God's economy in the believers' experience is
the processed Triune God. Without being processed, the
Triune God could not become grace. God is one, yet He is
three—the Father, the Son, and the Spirit. The Son is the
embodiment and expression of the Father, and the Spirit is
the reality and realization of the Son. In the Son the Father is
expressed and seen, and as the Spirit the Son is revealed and
realized. This Triune God dispenses Himself into us to be our
portion as grace to us that we may enjoy Him as our everything in His Divine Trinity.

A. God, Who Was in the Beginning,
Becoming Flesh in Time
as Grace for Man
to Receive, Possess, and Enjoy

God, who was in the beginning, became flesh in time as
grace for man to receive, possess, and enjoy (John 1:1, 14,
16-17). The first step, which is also the greatest step, of the
process which the Triune God passed through was incarnation. God, who was in the beginning, became flesh in time;
that was His tabernacling among men. His coming among
men in this way was full of grace, and of His fullness we have
all received. He came that we might receive grace, even grace
upon grace. When He came, grace also came. The law was
given to us, but grace came through Jesus Christ. The law
could not come by itself; hence, it was given to us, but grace

came with Jesus. Actually, grace is Jesus. When Jesus came, grace came. This is the Triune God with His divinity mingled into humanity becoming a God-man. Such a One is grace for us to receive, enjoy, and experience as our supply. This is the real salvation of the Lord.

It is amazing that one day the eternal God, the Creator of all things, was conceived in the womb of the virgin Mary. Not only so, but He stayed in the virgin's womb for nine months. The eternal God, the infinite God, the Creator of all things, entered into the womb of a little virgin and stayed there for nine months! In His creation, God ordained that there be nine months for a human pregnancy. God did not violate this principle. At the fullness of nine months, He came out of the mother's womb and became a child.

1. The Incarnated God Being Triune— the Father, the Son, and the Spirit

a. The Father as the Source Being Embodied and Expressed in the Son

The incarnated God is triune—the Father, the Son, and the Spirit (Matt. 28:19). The Father as the source is embodied and expressed in the Son (John 14:8-11). God the Father is hidden, and God the Son is manifested among men. The little child lying in the manger was the eternal God, the infinite Lord, and the Lord who created the heavens, the earth, and all things. The incarnated God has been united and mingled with man. He is both the complete God and the perfect man. He is a God-man. He remained in humanity and was mingled with humanity. This God-man passed through thirty-three and a half years of human living. In the first thirty years He lived in a poor carpenter's home and learned from Joseph to be a carpenter. He tasted and passed through all the hardships and pains of human life. Do not forget that this One who was a carpenter is the Creator of all things mingled with humanity as a small man.

At the fullness of thirty years He began to minister. He came out of Nazareth of Galilee, a despised place. He had no attracting form or majesty that people would desire Him, but

His words were with power, and His doings were with great might. He caused the blind to see, the lame to walk, the deaf to hear, the dumb to speak, and the dead to be raised. The words He spoke had never been spoken by anyone else. He said, "I am the way and the reality and the life" (John 14:6). He also said, "I have come that they may have life and may have it abundantly" (10:10b). These words are easy to understand, yet they are very profound. Neither Confucius nor Socrates spoke these words; they could not think of such words. The words of the so-called philosophers cannot be compared to the words of the Lord Jesus.

The Lord Jesus did many things and spoke many words on earth. Eventually, He was betrayed, arrested, and crucified on the cross. He was crucified from 9:00 A.M. until 3:00 P.M., suffering on the cross for six hours. During the first three hours He was persecuted by men for doing God's will; in the last three hours He was judged by God to accomplish our redemption. During this time God counted Him as our substitute, who took the place of sinners, bearing our sins and being made sin for us. Hence, God forsook Christ on the cross. About 3:00 P.M. Jesus cried out with a loud voice, saying, "My God, My God, why have You forsaken Me?" (Matt. 27:46). When He yielded up His spirit, the veil of the temple was split in two from top to bottom, the earth was shaken, and the rocks were split. Moreover, the tombs were opened, and many bodies of the saints who had fallen asleep were raised. They came out of the tombs after Jesus' resurrection and appeared to many. All these phenomena proved that His death was not an ordinary death. He died and was buried; on the third day He resurrected from the dead. On the day after the Sabbath, which was the first day of the week, while it was still dark, some sisters went to Jesus' tomb and were weeping there. Jesus appeared to them in resurrection, telling them, "Go to My brothers and say to them, I ascend to My Father and your Father, and My God and your God" (John 20:17). In the evening of that day He again appeared to the disciples and breathed into them, saying, "Receive the Holy Spirit" (v. 22).

b. The Son Being Realized as the Spirit
and Abiding in the Believers

In His resurrection He did a great thing—He was transfigured to become the Spirit. In His incarnation He as God was transformed to become a man. In His resurrection He as God in the flesh was transformed again to become the life-giving Spirit. The Father as the source is embodied and expressed in the Son; the Son is realized as the Spirit and abides in the believers (John 14:16-20). Now He is qualified to be our grace. Such a transformed One is grace. In the Bible the Lord Jesus is likened to a cake. A cake does not come about in a simple way. First, a grain of wheat falls into the ground, sprouts, and produces many grains after much suffering. Then the grains are ground and sifted into flour, which is mixed with water to form a cake. Finally, the cake has to be baked over the fire, and then it becomes ready to eat. This signifies that the Triune God has been processed into a "cake." This "cake" is grace. Today in His resurrection and in His ascension He transfuses Himself into us as a cake for our enjoyment. This is the process that the Triune God passed through in order to enter into man.

c. The Spirit Being in the Believers
as Their Life and Life Supply—
the Living Water of Life,
the Bread of Life, and the Breath of Life—
and Becoming the Divine Grace Enjoyed by Them

The Spirit is in the believers as their life and life supply—first, to be the living water of life for them to drink (John 7:37-39); second, to be the bread of life for them to eat (6:63); and third, to be the breath of life for them to breathe in (20:22). The Spirit also becomes the divine grace enjoyed by them. We experience Him as the living water, the bread of life, and the breath of life. The basic necessities for human existence are these three things—eating, drinking, and breathing. As far as our spiritual life is concerned, we need the living water of life, the bread of life, and the breath of life as our supply. By eating, drinking, and breathing we live and grow. Christ as the life-giving Spirit is God's transfiguration to be grace to us. This Spirit in us imparts the Triune God into us as grace, that is, as our living water, bread of life, and breath of life, to supply us that we may live and grow.

d. The Indwelling Spirit, the Processed Triune God, Abiding in the Believers as the Anointing and Becoming Their Enjoyment in Life

The indwelling Spirit, the processed Triune God, abides in the believers as the anointing and becomes their enjoyment in life (1 John 4:13; 2:27). The Spirit, whom God has given to dwell in us, is the witness in our spirit, witnessing that we dwell in God and God in us. The indwelling Spirit is the element and sphere of God's indwelling that we may experience and enjoy His abiding in us. The Spirit, who dwells in our spirit, is also the basic element of the divine anointing to be our enjoyment in life.

e. The Anointing Spirit, the Pneumatic Christ, the Spirit Who Speaks to the Churches, Eventually Becoming the Counterpart of the Church, the Bride

The anointing Spirit, the pneumatic Christ, the Spirit who speaks to the churches, eventually becomes the counterpart of the church, the bride (Rev. 2:1, 7; 22:17). We are His counterpart, and He also becomes our counterpart. The two become one couple with the same life, the same nature, and the same operation. Thus, we become His increase. John 3 says that those whom He has regenerated are His increase. His increase becomes His bride; His bride is His counterpart, a part of Him, as His Body; the Body is the temple of God; and the temple of God is the house of God. In chapter two of John His increase is the temple of God. Then in chapter fourteen it is the house of God. The temple, the house, is the tree in chapter fifteen that is full of branches as its increase. This is the Gospel of John. There is neither the thought of doing good or evil nor the concept of being right or wrong. There is only the organism as the product of the union and mingling of the Triune God with man. This is the issue of grace in us.

2. Such a Processed and Consummated Triune God Being the Grace Enjoyed by All the Believers in God's New Testament Economy, Even for Eternity

Such a processed and consummated Triune God is the grace enjoyed by all the believers in God's New Testament economy, even for eternity (Rev. 22:21). In the Gospel of John there is neither right and wrong nor good and evil. In the garden of Eden, before man had eaten of the tree of the knowledge of good and evil, man had no concept of good and evil. Man had only one concept—to receive God. The man created by God had God's inward image and outward likeness. In creating man, God gave man a thought, that is, to have God. God is man's unique concept. It is not a matter of doing good or doing evil, but a matter of having God or not having God. However, Satan came in and tempted man to eat of the tree of the knowledge of good and evil, which is anything other than the tree of life. As soon as man ate of the tree of the knowledge of good and evil, the concept of good and evil entered into him. From that time to this day, fallen human beings, including Christians and even those who are in the Lord's recovery, are often concerned about good or evil and right or wrong. We like to ask, "Is it right? Is it right for the elders to do this? Is it right for the deacons to do that?" Whether it is right or wrong, it does not matter; it is just a "photo." The Pentateuch is full of what is right, what is wrong, what is good, and what is evil, but the Gospel of John is not. The Gospel of John tells us that the Word, who was in the beginning, became flesh in time that divinity and humanity may be united and mingled together into a God-man. This God-man does not care about right or wrong, nor about good or evil. All He cares about is that you receive the grace that He brought. Today it is not enough to say, as the inner-life people do, that what God wants is neither good nor evil but Christ. This kind of speaking is very good, but it does not touch the main point. Actually, God does not want you to live; He wants you to take Him as life and live by Him.

In Galatians 2:20 Paul says, "I am crucified with Christ;

and it is no longer I who live, but it is Christ who lives in me; and the life which I now live in the flesh I live in faith, the faith of the Son of God." This means that now I live, but it is not I living alone, not I living by myself; it is Christ and I living in union. I now live, but it is no longer I, yet I still live; and the life which I now live is the life I live in union with Christ. Concerning this matter, even the inner-life people do not have a clear vision. It is not that we do not move; we still move and therefore we can live Christ and magnify Christ. If we are no more, how can we magnify Christ? It is not that we are no more; we still live. However, we do not take the initiative; we take Him as our initiative. It is in this way that we live Christ and magnify Christ.

The Christian life is Christ living and I also living, yet it is not I bringing Him along to live with me, but His bringing me along to live with Him. I am living along with Him, taking Him as my life and person. Dear brothers and sisters, if you take Him as your life and person, that is, He lives and you live along with Him, can you still lose your temper? Will you still try to do good? Will you still try to love others? All these concepts will vanish. You will have only one concept—He moves, and you move along with Him; He is your life and your person; you take Him as your life and your person; He is your inward life and your outward living. There is no concept of whether or not to honor your parents, nor any concept of whether or not to steal. You are altogether in another world. This is a world in which the Triune God is your life and your person, a world in which you live by Him—He is taking the lead and you are going along—and a world in which He lives and you live with Him, not living by yourself. I hope that we all can see this. If the older ones, the younger ones, the elders, the deacons, and the co-workers in the church all can see this, there will be no more arguments.

The arguments in the church all come from being right or wrong, from the tree of the knowledge of good and evil. We can find out concerning what is right and what is wrong in the Pentateuch but not in the Gospel of John; all that the Gospel of John has is life. Christ is my life and my person—He lives and I also live; He moves and I also move; it

is not I but He who takes the initiative. I am His counterpart;
I am a part of His Body. What is right or what is not right is
not the concern of the Body of Christ.

B. With the Love, the Grace, and the Fellowship of the Divine Trinity as Factors

The grace in God's economy in the believers' experience is
the processed Triune God with the love, the grace, and the fellowship of the Divine Trinity as factors (2 Cor. 13:14).

1. With the Love of God the Father, Who Is over All and through All and in All, as the Source

In the love, the grace, and the fellowship of the Divine
Trinity, the love of God the Father, who is over all and
through all and in all, is the source (Eph. 4:6; 2 Cor. 13:14b).
We say that the Triune God is mingled with us, but some do
not receive this word. On the contrary, they say that God can
be united with us but not mingled with us. I would ask, then,
why it says here that God the Father is over us, through us,
and in us? Is this merely a union? This is not merely a union;
it is mingling.

2. With the Grace of God the Son, Who Abides in the Believers and Makes His Home in Their Hearts, as the Element

In the love, the grace, and the fellowship of the Divine
Trinity, the grace of God the Son, who abides in the believers
and makes His home in their hearts, is the element (John
15:5; Eph. 3:17; 2 Cor. 13:14a). The love of the Father is the
source, whereas the grace of the Son is the element.

3. With the Fellowship of God the Spirit, Who Dwells in the Believers and Is Mingled with Their Spirit as One Spirit, as the Distribution

In the love, the grace, and the fellowship of the Divine
Trinity, the fellowship of God the Spirit, who dwells in the
believers and is mingled with their spirit as one spirit, is the
distribution (Rom. 8:11, 16; 2 Cor. 13:14b). The Father is
the source, the Son is the element, and the Spirit distributes

the Triune God into us that we may take Him as our life and our person to live out His image and express Him.

II. THE NEW TESTAMENT BELIEVERS' LIVING UNDER THE GRACE IN GOD'S ECONOMY BEING A TOTAL LIVING OF EXPERIENCING THE PROCESSED TRIUNE GOD AS GRACE

The New Testament believers' living under the grace in God's economy is a total living of experiencing the processed Triune God as grace. It is not a matter of what to do; that is not a total living. A total living means that my entire living is a living of the Triune God processed to be grace in me. It is not a matter of whether or not to judge others; that is not a total living but a fragmented living. A total living means that twenty-four hours a day, whether I am awake or asleep, I take the Triune God as my life and my person. I follow His move; I move with Him. Two spirits become one spirit, two lives live together, and two natures are mingled together. This is the total living of experiencing the Triune God as grace. A total living is not the living concerning right and wrong, good and evil, or anything else, but the living of a living person. The living of this living person is the mingled living of the processed Triune God with the tripartite transformed man. Thus, God becomes our grace, and we live in this grace. This is the grace referred to in the New Testament. Our experience of the grace in God's economy is the mutual living of the processed Triune God and us joined together, taking Him as our life and person. He initiates, and we follow; He and we move together to live out a certain condition, which is called an organism, to express God Himself. Here, there is no concept of right and wrong or good and evil. The law is a photo of God for the old covenant, whereas grace is God Himself. We do not care for the photo; we care for the living person.

A. The Processed Triune God, Consummated as the All-inclusive, Life-giving, Compound, and Indwelling Spirit, Becoming the Spirit of Grace

The processed Triune God, who has been consummated as the all-inclusive, life-giving, compound, and indwelling

Spirit, becomes the Spirit of grace (1 Cor. 15:45b; 2 Cor. 3:17; Rev. 22:17a; Heb. 10:29).

1. In the New Testament Age the Spirit of Grace Dispensing the Triune God into the Believers as Grace

In the New Testament age the Spirit of grace dispenses the Triune God into the believers as grace. Since the Spirit of grace dispenses the Triune God into us to be our grace, our Christian life is essentially a life of having God as our grace.

2. At the End of the New Testament Age the Spirit of Grace Causing the Whole House of Israel to Repent and Receive the Triune God as Grace

At the end of the New Testament age, the Spirit of grace will cause the whole house of Israel to repent and receive the Triune God as grace. Zechariah 12:10 says that God will pour out the Spirit of grace upon the remnant of Israel that the whole house of Israel may repent and be saved.

B. The Compound, Life-giving Spirit and the Believers' Regenerated Spirit Becoming One Mingled Spirit

The compound, life-giving Spirit and the believers' regenerated spirit become one mingled spirit (Rom. 8:4b-6), not only united but also mingled.

C. The Believers' Living and Work by the Spirit, Essentially and Economically, Being Their Experience and Enjoyment of the Pneumatic Christ, the Embodiment of the Triune God, as Grace

Both essentially and economically, that is, both in their living and in their moving, the believers' living and work by the Spirit is the experience and enjoyment of the pneumatic

Christ, the embodiment of the Triune God, as grace (John 1:14, 16; Rev. 22:21).

The Triune God passed through a process from His being merely God without humanity to His entering into humanity and being mingled with humanity as one. Then He passed through human living and an all-inclusive death and entered into the all-producing resurrection, producing the firstborn Son of God, the many sons of God, and the life-giving Spirit. This One who was in resurrection also entered into ascension and became the all-inclusive life-giving Spirit, who is typified by the holy anointing oil in Exodus 30:22-25. The holy anointing oil is the fragrant olive oil compounded with four kinds of spices. It is not merely oil but an ointment with various elements. This is a type of the compound Spirit, in whom are the Father and the Son with His all-inclusive death, His human living, His resurrection, and His ascension. Now the compound Spirit is moving within us daily as the anointing that we may enjoy the processed Triune God as grace. This is the life that we Christians should have today.

CHAPTER FOUR

THE CONSUMMATION
OF THE BELIEVERS' EXPERIENCE
OF THE GRACE OF GOD IN HIS ECONOMY

Scripture Reading: Eph. 1:6-8, 22-23; 1 Cor. 3:12; Rev. 21:18-21a; John 17:11, 21-23; Eph. 4:3-4a; 1 Cor. 1:13a; Eph. 2:7, 10

OUTLINE

I. The consummation being the church as the Body of Christ—Eph. 1:6-8, 22-23:
   A. As the organism which God in His economy intends to obtain for the Divine Trinity.
   B. As the ultimate goal of God's creation of man in His image and His intention for man to take Him as life.
   C. As the final purpose of the law of God in His economy in guarding God's chosen people and bringing them to Christ.
   D. As the accomplishment of man's experience of the grace in the economy of God, which is Himself as the processed Triune God, ultimately consummating in the New Jerusalem.

II. Every part of the organic Body of Christ being an issue of the grace in the economy of God:
   A. With God the Father in His nature as its substance, as pure gold—1 Cor. 3:12; Rev. 21:18b.
   B. With God the Son in His redemption as its element, as pearls—1 Cor. 3:12; Rev. 21:21a.
   C. With God the Spirit in His transforming work as

its essence, as precious stones—1 Cor. 3:12; Rev. 21:18a, 19-20.

   D. Having absolutely neither man's natural element nor man's work by his own effort.

III. The organism of the Divine Trinity taking the attribute of the oneness of the Divine Trinity as its attribute:

   A. The unique attribute of the Divine Trinity being oneness—John 17:11, 21a, 22b.

   B. In the unique attribute of the Divine Trinity the organism of the Divine Trinity also having the same unique attribute—John 17:21b, 22b-23.

   C. The attribute of the oneness of the Divine Trinity being called the oneness of the Spirit in the organic Body of Christ—Eph. 4:3-4a.

   D. The creating of any divisions in the organic Body of Christ being an insult to and a contempt for the Triune God, whose attribute is oneness—cf. 1 Cor. 1:13a.

IV. The product of the grace in God's economy being a poem—Eph. 2:10a:

   A. To exhibit the surpassing riches of the grace in God's economy—Eph. 2:7.

   B. To carry out the good works that God prepared beforehand that the believers may walk in—Eph. 2:10b.

Prayer: O Lord, we worship You. For Your economy and Your speaking, we worship You. We bow down to You from the depths of our being. You are the Lord who speaks. You speak words to us with enlightening revelation and life supply. O Lord, as we come to the final message, we pray that You would speak thoroughly and completely. We also pray that You would reach every one of us with Your words that we may all hear Your speaking. O Lord Jesus, as the speaking God, You are the Word of God; we worship You. May You touch every one of us in our depths and sow every word of Yours into us. O Lord, cleanse us with Your precious blood; we need Your cleansing every day. We have the filthiness of our natural being, the filthiness of our flesh, the filthiness of our lusts, and the filthiness of the earth. Lord, all these need the cleansing of Your precious blood in every way. We thank and praise You that Your precious blood is always accompanied by the anointing. After the cleansing of the blood, we enjoy the anointing of the ointment. We believe that Your ointment is here anointing us. Once more we ask You to give us utterance and grant us fresh and up-to-date words. Amen.

In this message we come to the conclusion, which is the consummation of the believers' experience of the grace of God in His economy. In the course of carrying out His economy, God first handed down the law. The law is His portrait, His image, His "photo"; it is not His organic person. Galatians 3:21 tells us that the law cannot give life because there is no life in the law. Although a photo cannot give life, it has its function. The law in God's economy is used by God to expose sinners in their sinful nature and evil deeds. Before His law all mouths are shut. We have violated, broken, every commandment of the Ten Commandments, from the first one to the last one. We have had numerous idols apart from God. We have not taken God as our satisfaction, neither have we taken what He has accomplished for us as our rest. Rather, we have forsaken God as the fountain of living waters to hew out for ourselves cisterns, broken cisterns, which hold no water (Jer. 2:13). We have not traced back to our beginning, our origin, to honor our source—the very God who created us. Furthermore, our hearts have been filled with murder, adultery, stealing, lying, and coveting. We have not lived out God's outward virtues according to His inward attributes.

David was a very devout person. In Psalm 1 he related how he appreciated the law and meditated in it by day and by night like a tree planted beside streams of water. However, after David's word of appreciation in Psalm 1, God repudiated David's concept and announced concerning His Anointed, "You are My Son; / Today I have begotten You" (2:7b). In resurrection God has begotten His Anointed as His firstborn Son. God's desire is that we listen to His anointed Firstborn instead of appreciating the law. Psalm 3 was written by David in his flight from his son Absalom's rebellion, which was the outcome of David's sin of murder and robbing a man of his wife. In Psalm 1, David was one who appreciated the law, yet in Psalm 3 he was fleeing from his rebellious son as a consequence of his murder and robbing a man of his wife. The result of David's appreciation of the law was murder and robbing a man of his wife. The law of God fully uncovered David's sinful nature and evil deeds. The entire book of one hundred fifty psalms shows us that the law is used by God to expose man in his sinful nature and evil deeds.

Now the New Testament believers in God's economy are not under law but under grace. The grace in God's economy is God's embodiment. God became flesh to dwell among us, full of grace, and of His fullness we have all received, and grace upon grace. When God comes, grace comes. God's embodiment is grace to us. When we receive grace, we obtain God.

God's economy is to work out an organism for the Divine Trinity. How does He work this out? It is by His becoming flesh to be a man that His divinity and humanity might be united and mingled to produce a God-man. This God-man is grace. Whomever He meets, He is grace to them; wherever He goes, He is grace. He is simply grace. If we have Him, we have grace. Hence, in the Bible grace is called the grace of Christ. The embodied grace came for us to receive as our enjoyment and supply. However, there are few who see this today, even fewer who preach this, and very few who live this out.

If we experience the grace in God's economy, there will be a consummation—the organic Body of Christ. Christ to us is grace; as such, He comes into us to be our life and person. He not only lives in us but also lives with us. Moreover, He wants us to live along with Him. This is to enjoy grace as our inner supply. Such an enjoyment of grace spontaneously produces a result. This result is not merely that we do good. Rather, it is that Christ lives with us and we with Him. When we live Christ and magnify Christ, we become the living members, organic members, of Christ, and we all are organically joined as an organism, which is the church. This organism grows continually, and ultimately there will be a consummation—the New Jerusalem.

The last stanza of *Hymns,* #840 says,

> In God's house and in Thy Body
>   Builded up I long to be,
> That within this corporate vessel
>   All shall then Thy glory see;
> That Thy Bride, the glorious city,
>   May appear upon the earth,
> As a lampstand brightly beaming
>   To express to all Thy worth.

Christianity has not seen this, and accordingly, they do not have such a result. I expect that in the Lord's recovery there will be such a possibility and such an expression. This is my burden, and this is why I grieve. Today there are many arguments and discussions, but there are not many who have seen this vision. If you see this vision, you will weep. Where is "the glorious city" today? "That Thy Bride, the glorious city, may appear upon the earth"—is this possible? Are we enjoying grace and the supply of grace? May the Lord have mercy upon us. We are a group of people who really need His mercy. We should be a group of people who experience and enjoy grace in our living and in our words and actions. This grace is God's embodiment that we supply to others that they also may receive grace with us. As a result, our experience has a consummation—the Body of Christ.

I. THE CONSUMMATION BEING THE CHURCH
AS THE BODY OF CHRIST

The consummation of the believers' experience of the grace of God in His economy is the church as the Body of Christ (Eph. 1:6-8, 22-23). How is the Body of Christ produced? We were fallen sinners, but Christ came and shed His blood to redeem us back into Himself. Christ is the sphere and element of our salvation. The precious blood of Christ redeemed us back into Himself as the sphere and element. In Christ we enjoy His element, and with His element we have been made God's precious possession. Ephesians 1:22-23 shows us that the power that God caused to operate in Christ raised Him from the dead that He might transcend the world and ascend to the heavenlies, being seated on the right hand of God, crushing the enemy, having all things subjected under His feet, and thus being given to be the Head over all things. Such power is "to the church," that is, transmitted to the church. The church as His Body receives the transmission of this power. Since the Head has this power, the Body also receives the transmission of this power. It is in this way that the Body of Christ is produced.

A. As the Organism Which God in His Economy Intends to Obtain for the Divine Trinity

The church is the organism which God in His economy intends to obtain for the Divine Trinity. If today the glory of the bride, the holy city, is manifested, that is the appearing of the divine organism.

B. As the Ultimate Goal
of God's Creation of Man in His Image
and His Intention for Man to Take Him as Life

The Body of Christ is the ultimate goal of God's creation of man in His image and His intention for man to take Him as life. This was the ultimate goal in Genesis 2. Genesis 2 shows us that after man was created in the image of God, God put man in front of the tree of life that man might take in God's life, signified by the tree of life. Thus, man would have God's image and God's life to live out God and become His organism. However, six thousand years have gone by, and to this day God has not obtained His ultimate goal.

C. As the Final Purpose of the Law of God in His Economy in Guarding God's Chosen People and Bringing Them to Christ

The Body of Christ is the final purpose of the law of God in His economy in guarding God's chosen people and bringing them to Christ. Even the law of God in His economy was in expectation of the final purpose—the Body of Christ. Although God used the law to expose people, it was with the expectation that the law would give way to grace and attain the final purpose through grace. Otherwise, why would the law keep God's chosen people under its custody and serve as their conductor to bring them to Christ as grace? The law has a positive function before God, and that is to bring us to Christ, to grace. This was David's experience. When we read Psalm 51, a psalm of his confession of sin, we can see that he knew grace and was clear concerning grace to a considerable extent. Who brought him to grace? It was the law. Originally, he appreciated the law, delighted in the law, and was confident that he could keep the law. At that time he did not know himself, but the law came and exposed his sinful nature and evil deeds. After being rebuked by God, he repented and was brought to grace.

D. As the Accomplishment of Man's Experience of the Grace in the Economy of God, Which Is Himself as the Processed Triune God, Ultimately Consummating in the New Jerusalem

The Body of Christ is also the accomplishment of man's experience of the grace in the economy of God, which is Himself as the processed Triune God, ultimately consummating in the New Jerusalem. *Hymns,* #979 is a sweet hymn on the many characteristics of the holy city, the New Jerusalem. For the last two thousand years, ordinary Bible readers and even Bible scholars have been puzzled by the New Jerusalem, wondering whether it is a material city or whether it refers to something else. Because of man's natural concept according

to human understanding, most consider the New Jerusalem a
material city. I still remember that when I was young, I sang
a hymn that says one day we will enter the golden city with a
golden street, pearl gates, and a jasper wall. But within my
heart I said, "Did the Lord die and shed His blood just to save
me into a golden city?" From then on I began to pursue to
know what the New Jerusalem really is. Eventually, around
1960 I saw clearly that this city is not a physical city but a
sign to express a spiritual reality that cannot be expressed
with ordinary words. God began to use such signs in Genesis 2, where there is the tree of life. In the New Testament the
tree of life reappears. In Revelation 2:7 the Lord says, "To
him who overcomes, to him I will give to eat of the tree of life,
which is in the Paradise of God." At the end of Revelation, the
tree of life is again present in the New Jerusalem (22:2).
Based upon this, I made a bold judgment that the New Jerusalem is a sign, because the tree of life within the city is a
sign. Since that tree is not a physical tree but a sign, the city
must also be a sign.

Furthermore, Revelation 21:22 says that there is no
temple in the city of the New Jerusalem. What is the temple?
The temple is God and the Lamb as the place for God's people
to worship God and enjoy God. Therefore, the temple is also a
sign. It is not a real building within the city; rather, God and
the Lamb are the temple. Furthermore, Revelation 21:23
says, "The city has no need of the sun or of the moon that they
should shine in it, for the glory of God illumined it, and its
lamp is the Lamb." Both the lamp and the light refer to God's
glory. Therefore, both the lamp and the light are signs, not
physical things. Moreover, in the New Jerusalem Christ is
the Lamb. This surely does not mean that Christ in the New
Jerusalem is a lamb with four legs and a tail. The Lamb is a
sign. In addition, the New Jerusalem is the tabernacle of God
(v. 3). Eventually, the city will become a tabernacle; this is
also a sign. On the one hand, it is a city with gates, founda-
tions, and a wall; on the other hand, it is the tabernacle of
God—the place where God dwells with man. Finally, this city
is the bride, the wife of the Lamb (v. 2). All these indicate that
the entire holy city, the New Jerusalem, is not a physical city;

rather, it is the ultimate sign, the greatest sign in the Bible, signifying the aggregate, the totality, of the redeemed saints throughout the generations, who have been regenerated, transformed, and glorified, as the consummation of man's experience of the Triune God, which is the organic Body of Christ.

II. EVERY PART OF THE ORGANIC BODY OF CHRIST BEING AN ISSUE OF THE GRACE IN THE ECONOMY OF GOD

Every part of the organic Body of Christ is an issue of the grace in the economy of God. Grace is the enjoyment of the Triune God—the Father, the Son, and the Spirit—as the enjoyment of life, and the life of God is with God the Father as the substance, God the Son as the element, and God the Spirit as the essence.

A. With God the Father in His Nature as Its Substance, as Pure Gold

First, the organic Body of Christ takes God the Father in His nature as its substance, as pure gold (1 Cor. 3:12; Rev. 21:18b). Gold signifies the divine nature of God the Father as the source with all its attributes.

B. With God the Son in His Redemption as Its Element, as Pearls

Second, the organic Body of Christ takes God the Son in His redemption as its element, as pearls (1 Cor. 3:12; Rev. 21:21a). Pearls signify Christ the Son in His overcoming death and life-imparting resurrection with all the virtues and attributes.

C. With God the Spirit in His Transforming Work as Its Essence, as Precious Stones

Third, the organic Body of Christ takes God the Spirit in His transforming work as its essence, as precious stones (1 Cor. 3:12; Rev. 21:18a, 19-20). Precious stones signify the transforming work of the Spirit with all its attributes. Gold, silver, and precious stones signify the believers' various enjoyments and experiences of Christ in the virtues and attributes of the Triune God. All these precious materials are the products of our participation in and enjoyment of Christ in our spirit through the Holy Spirit. Only these are good for God's building.

The organic Body of Christ, which is the church, is produced through the redeemed and regenerated saints' experience of transformation by the consummated Triune God—the Spirit. Hence, we need to be filled with the Spirit, the essence of the Divine Trinity. Today the Spirit is the all-inclusive life-giving Spirit, and He is the realization of Christ. Christ, the last Adam, after passing through an all-inclusive death, became the life-giving Spirit in resurrection as the essence of the Divine Trinity to come into us to be our life and everything. Day by day we need to be filled with Him, saturated with Him, permeated by Him, infused by Him, and transfused by Him. Hence, as we read the New Testament, we cannot avoid the word *Spirit*. Especially in the Epistles, the emphasis is on the Spirit, and the Spirit is frequently linked with grace. When we teach and shepherd others, we do not exhort them to do something; that is the way of religion, not the Spirit. We need to be filled with the Spirit, the essence of the Divine Trinity, that our mind may become more sober, our will may become more firm, and our emotion may be filled with love. When we have the Spirit in us, we have the essence of the Triune God in us.

The Triune God passed through various processes. He became flesh, lived a human life, and passed through an all-inclusive death. With Adam, death is not good, but with Christ, death is very precious. The death of Christ, like today's antibiotics, kills all the germs. Christ's death terminated the old creation, the flesh, the old man, sin, Satan, the world, the ordinances, the commandments, and all the different customs in human living. Christ's death also released the divine life from within Him. From this death He entered into the life-generating power, which is resurrection. In this resurrection He was begotten to be God's firstborn Son. Originally, He was God's only begotten Son without humanity. After His incarnation, because His flesh, His humanity, was not the Son of God, He had to pass through resurrection and be "sonized." Now He is no longer merely the only begotten Son of God; He is also the firstborn Son of God. In eternity past He was the only begotten Son of God, having divinity but not humanity. Now in resurrection He was begotten to be the firstborn Son of God, having both divinity and humanity. Furthermore, in His resurrection He regenerated us that we may be born as children of God. He is God's firstborn Son, and we are God's many sons. In resurrection He was also transfigured into the life-giving Spirit. In eternity past He did not have all these items, but He passed through the various processes and became the all-inclusive, compound, indwelling, life-giving Spirit. This Spirit is the consummated Triune God, the processed Triune God, who is available for us to eat, drink, and enjoy. He Himself said that He is edible and that he who eats Him shall live because of Him (John 6:57).

D. Having Absolutely Neither Man's Natural Element nor Man's Work by His Own Effort

The organic Body of Christ has absolutely neither man's natural element nor man's work by his own effort. Originally, we were men of clay; however, in the New Jerusalem there is no clay but gold, pearls, and precious stones. Since gold signifies God's divine nature, the New Jerusalem's being of pure gold signifies that the New Jerusalem is altogether of God's divine nature and takes God's divine nature as its element. Pearls are produced by oysters in the waters of death. This signifies that Christ came into the death waters, was wounded by us, and secreted His life over us to make us into precious pearls. Precious stones are not created but are produced by the transforming of things created. We were created as clay, but after we have passed through the intense heat and pressure of the work of the Holy Spirit in us and in our environment, we are transformed into precious stones good for God's eternal building.

We all need to pass through regeneration and transformation, and then we can become a part of the New Jerusalem. In His economy God arranges the persons, things, and events

around us in a wonderful way that we may learn the lessons
of being burned and pressed and thereby transformed in life.
Whether in the church life or in the family life, we all have
experienced such burning and pressing. If we have not been
burned and pressed, we remain natural wood, grass, and
stubble and cannot be precious stones for building. In order to
become precious stones we need to be transformed. Whether
at home or in the church, once we begin to quarrel, the fire is
extinguished and the pressure is gone. Then, we are all natural materials, not transformed materials for the building.

If we are not willing to be transformed by being burned or
pressed today, we will not be able to enter the New Jerusalem. In His economy God sets aside the millennial kingdom
as a reward to the transformed and overcoming believers. If
we are transformed in life by receiving the Spirit's exercise
and God's discipline today, we will be rewarded by the Lord at
His coming back—we will receive the reward of the kingdom
and enter into its glory. The believers who are not willing to
have the transformation in life by receiving the Spirit's exercise and God's discipline will be cast into outer darkness at
the Lord's coming, where they will regret with weeping and
gnashing of teeth. Today's burning and pressing are, at most,
for one hundred years, but in the future, the burning and
pressing will be ten times greater, lasting a thousand years.
This is the clear revelation of the Bible. Heaven and earth
will pass away, but every iota and every serif of the words in
the Scriptures shall by no means pass away (Matt. 5:18). The
overcomers will reign with Christ in the millennial kingdom
and receive the sonship. Furthermore, they will serve God
and Christ as royal priests in the glory of Christ's appearing.
The overcomers will already be precious stones in the millennium, whereas the defeated ones as the natural materials
that have not been transformed will be in the darkness, weeping and gnashing their teeth. After the millennium, all the
saved ones will eventually be in the New Jerusalem in the
new heaven and new earth. However, during the millennium,
only the overcomers will be in the New Jerusalem, and the
defeated ones will not be there.

III. THE ORGANISM OF THE DIVINE TRINITY TAKING THE ATTRIBUTE OF THE ONENESS OF THE DIVINE TRINITY AS ITS ATTRIBUTE

The organism of the Divine Trinity takes the attribute of the oneness of the Divine Trinity as its attribute. The Lord's words in John 17 clearly show us that the unique attribute of the Divine Trinity is oneness. Since the unique attribute of the Divine Trinity is oneness, the unique attribute of the organism of the Divine Trinity must also be oneness. If we are in discord with the members of the Body of Christ, we are not in this oneness and are in contradiction to the unique attribute of this organism.

The unique attribute of the Divine Trinity is oneness (John 17:11, 21b, 22b). In such a unique attribute of the Divine Trinity, the organism of the Divine Trinity also possesses the same unique attribute (v. 21a, 22b-23). This oneness as the attribute of the Divine Trinity is called the oneness of the Spirit in the organic Body of Christ (Eph. 4:3-4a). In the organic Body of Christ, the creating of any divisions is an insult to and a contempt for the Triune God, whose attribute is oneness (cf. 1 Cor. 1:13a). To create divisions is to blaspheme God. Hence, in Romans 16:16-17 Paul is unyielding and resolute in saying that we should mark those who are dissenting, who make divisions, and who make causes of stumbling, and that we should turn away from them. In this organism there cannot be divisions. The essential attribute of this organism is oneness.

IV. THE PRODUCT OF THE GRACE IN GOD'S ECONOMY BEING A POEM

The product of the grace in God's economy is a poem (Eph. 2:10a). The heavens, the earth, and man, which were created by God, are not God's poem. Rather, the church, the Body of Christ, is God's poem.

A. To Exhibit the Surpassing Riches of the Grace in God's Economy

The product of the grace in God's economy is a poem to exhibit the surpassing riches of the grace in God's economy

(Eph. 2:7). These riches in their many aspects are referred to again and again in the New Testament, especially in the Epistles written by the apostle Paul. Grace is rich, abounding, multiplying, and increasing.

B. To Carry Out the Good Works That God Prepared Beforehand for the Believers to Walk In

We have been saved by the surpassing and rich grace that we may carry out the good works that God prepared beforehand for us to walk in (Eph. 2:10b). The good works for which God created us are not the good things that are according to our general concept, but the definite good doings that God preplanned and preordained for us to carry out while we are living in His organism. On the one hand, we are to exhibit the rich grace of God, and on the other hand, we are to carry out what God foreordained. These good works must be the doing of His will that we may live the church life and bear the testimony of Jesus Christ.

CONCLUSION

Now that we have seen the things covered in these four messages, I would ask you to examine and consider our condition today. May the Lord be merciful to us. Where are we? What is grace to us? To the apostle Paul, all things were like refuse, and grace was God in Christ. It was by grace, the Lord whom he experienced, that he labored for the Lord more abundantly than all the apostles. Like Paul, we should take the processed and consummated Triune God as grace in our living and work today. Our total living should be like this, not just doing some proper things or good things. In such a total living, it is altogether not a matter of being right or wrong or of doing good or evil; it is altogether in the sphere of the processed Triune God. In such a living we only take life as the principle. Whatever is of life, that is what God wants; whatever is not of life, that is what God rejects. This life is the rich grace with God the Father as the substance, God the Son as the element, and God the Spirit as the essence; this life is God coming to be our grace. This is the living that we should have. May the Lord be merciful to us and bless us that we may live such a life so that eventually we can experience the consummation of the grace of God in His economy.